Norton's
Philosophical
Memoirs

Håkan Nesser is a Swedish author and
teacher who has written a number of
successful books. He has won the Best
Swedish Crime Novel Award three times,
and the Glass Key Award in 2000. His
books have been translated into more
than twenty languages.

Norton's Philosophical Memoirs

Authored by Norton Kierkegaard
Transcribed by Håkan Nesser

Illustrated by Karin Hagen

Translated from the Swedish by Paul Norlen

ANIMA

an imprint of Head of Zeus

First published in Swedish in 2017 by Brombergs Bokförlag
First published in the UK in 2018 by Anima,
an imprint of Head of Zeus Ltd

9 7 5 3 1 2 4 6 8

A catalogue record for this book is available
from the British Library.

ISBN (HB): 9781786699770
ISBN (E): 9781786699763

Typeset by Adrian McLaughlin
Printed and bound in Germany by CPI Books GmbH

Head of Zeus Ltd
First Floor East
5–8 Hardwick Street
London ECIR 4RG
WWW.HEADOFZEUS.COM

CONTENTS

I. *Stages on Life's Way*
(2004–9)

Including: *The Man on the Moor* —
A Story from Real Life

OVERTURE

Now don't start getting ideas.

I am not a philosopher. I'm a dog.

But I *look* like a philosopher, they say, and I'm not sure the distinction is as great as you might think. In which case, the main difference is probably that we dogs keep our musings to ourselves. For good and ill.

I'm what's known as a Rhodesian ridgeback. My forebears used to hunt lions in Africa, but I'm a modernized urban specimen. I don't hunt much of anything. As I write this I happen to be with the man in an inn on a moor in England. It's not the moor of the Baskervilles; this one's called Exmoor, located right next to it.

I'm going to tell you something that happened yesterday. Firstly, because it's an instructive story, and secondly because I actually remember it; my memory isn't world class, truth be told. But we'll deal with that in due course. Let me start from the beginning, which is always a good idea.

PORTRAIT OF THE AUTHOR
AS A YOUNG PUP

I was born somewhere on the plains west of Uppsala, Sweden, but I don't remember much of that. In the beginning I was blind and tumbled around with my siblings. We pooped and bit each other and nursed, and our mother – who I must admit was kind of a bitch – tried to raise us to the best of her ability. Without all that much success, I must say.

Little by little our eyes opened, but there wasn't much to see other than the family during that early period. We lived in an extreme version of 'compact living' and I remember thinking that if it doesn't get any better than this, I should rather have been born in Africa twenty generations ago. However, it has to be noted that we did get food and water and all our basic needs were met.

When I was about two months old I was adopted. Two long-legged humans, a man and a woman, came and picked me up, loaded me in a car and drove into town. When I say 'town' I mean Uppsala. Their apartment was nice and big, but at first I pretty much stayed on a pad underneath the worktop in the kitchen. Whenever I needed to pee they picked me up and carried me out to the yard, and I figured out that the outdoors was really the toilet. For both one thing and the other.

There were a few good spots in that apartment. A big, soft footstool with a sheepskin on it, for example; I spent much of my first year on that. Likewise in a brown leather armchair where I could sit and look out over a river. It was called Fyris, I found out later, and it was quite sluggish. But it suited my temperament; I am a particularly calm philosopher, I mean dog, especially when I'm indoors. I can sleep up to fifteen hours a day and even when I'm awake I prefer to lie quite still. Some people think I'm stuffed, but that's not the case.

One of the differences between philosophers and dogs is that the latter are rather fond of being outdoors. But not to excess; a few hours a day is more than enough. My new people realized this; they had probably read a dog book or two, as I virtually didn't need to explain anything to them. Every day one of them loaded me in the car and then we drove out into the forest. Various wooded areas fifteen minutes or half an hour away from town, as I estimated it. Right from the start I liked to ride in cars and that was probably lucky considering my further adventures and fate.

Sometimes a friend went with me on those forest walks. He was a German shepherd and his name was Kastor. To start with it was all good, we raised all kinds of hell in among the trees, moss, sticks and twigs whirling as we rushed past, but when Kastor got a little older his temperament got a little worse. We snapped at each other a few times, there was bloodshed and more, and unfortunately I discovered that he was stronger than me.

It was roughly at this phase of my life that I decided
to become a pacifist. That isn't so common among us
philosophers, sorry, I mean dogs, but I would say that
I constitute a good benchmark. I am never aggressive
at all, not in the slightest. Even when my long-legged
caretakers suddenly showed up with a cat, Nelson,
I stayed calm. In time we became really good friends,
Nelson and I, even if he was pretty dim, let me tell
you. I write *was*, because Nelson has moved to
another family at this point. He had a tangled love
story in New York a little later in life, but I'm getting
ahead of myself.

MY UNIVERSITIES

The long-legged ones put me in a kind of class that first year. It was an incredibly dreary affair. There were ten or so of us youngsters who were supposed to learn to do all the things we didn't want to do. Run hither and thither on command, or sit still or lie down or fetch sticks and God knows what. Thank heavens class ended after only a month, and I must say that education in general is an overrated concept.

That family I lived with was not only made up of the tall man, the tall woman and silly Nelson. There was a slightly shorter young woman too, and someone whose name was Johannes. For a long time I didn't know whether he was a human or a dog. He was no philosopher anyway, but we had a lot of fun. We wrestled and tumbled around and bit each other, but then he moved to Stockholm and became an ice hockey player. The shorter younger woman was also gone on and off, but in later years she came back.

During the daily forest walks I learned a few things. For one, that the man sometimes gets lost, but that

he always seems to find his way back to the car. One doesn't really need to go and search for him, not even when he stands there calling one's name, forlornly. It's just as well that he learns how to handle things on his own; I don't want to spoil him.

They were rather calm and pleasant, those early years in Uppsala. I got a good foundation to stand on, you might say. But then one day, when I was approximately two and a half, the peaceful life came to an end. The big apartment by the river was emptied systematically of furniture, even my footstool and my pad disappeared, and anyone at all could figure out that a move was imminent.

Imagine my surprise anyway when we – the woman and I – drove off to a big airport, where I was stuffed into a cage and loaded on board an airplane. Luckily, I had my philosophical side to resort to; just in case, the woman drugged me a little too, so I did the only thing left to do while stuck in a crate: settled down and slept the whole eight-hour-long trip across the Atlantic.

When we got there it turned out that we were in America. Lazy Nelson had ridden with the woman inside the human compartment on the plane the whole way, and when I finally came out of the cage, the man was there to meet me. He had acquired a garishly painted camper van and explained that it would be our home for the next three months. Goodness gracious, I thought; you originate from Africa, you're born on the plains outside Uppsala in Sweden, and now you're going to roam about the United States of America too. The philosopher in me decided to become a Stoic.

AMERICA, EARLY ADULT YEARS

The big land in the West was not too bad, it turned out. It was hot, though, that whole summer, but I soon staked a claim to the passenger seat in the front next to the man, for he was usually the one who drove. There I could put my nose over the fresh-air intake, which was really pleasant. I of course had to deal with serving as map reader too, because that man is a marvel of un-technicality and had forgotten to acquire a GPS. When we drove into a new campground I usually had a straw hat and sunglasses on. 'Good God!' they would shout in reception. 'He looks like Sean Connery! What an excellent co-driver!' I think they figured out that we always got the best spot at the campground that way. In the evenings we lit a fire. Nelson and I were usually tied together with a clothesline; he had a tendency to disappear otherwise. Have I mentioned that he's not particularly bright? But there was undeniably something special about lying out there on the prairie in the glow of the campfire, faint country-western music from the neighbour's radio, occasionally you might even get a grilled piece of meat. But I never tried marshmallows. I have a somewhat sensitive stomach; it's not anything I'm ashamed of.

We roughed it for three months, through Minnesota, Michigan, Montana, Oregon, California and whatever they're called, those united states. Especially down south, in Louisiana and Florida and Georgia, it was as hot as in Africa, and I thought about my old ancestors as I sat there on the front seat reading the map. Perhaps it was just as well that they couldn't see me now: an African lion dog with a straw hat in a camper van. They wouldn't have believed their eyes; dogs are by nature usually a bit conservative.

Then suddenly one day the camper van was history. We found ourselves in a city with incredibly tall buildings and an unbelievable number of people. It was New York, I realized. We were going to live here, I understood too. Three flights up on a road called Carmine Street in an area called 'The Village'.

Well, well, I thought stoically. If they just get themselves a couch, I guess I'll put up with this too.

NEW YORK, NEW YORK

I was completely done in after a few days in that city. I know that my people thought I'd got sick. That wasn't the case, however; it was all to do with the smells.

There's another difference between philosophers and dogs that I haven't yet touched on. We dogs – though not completely indifferent to language – rely completely on our olfactory senses, which is of great delight and benefit to us, though sometimes it's more of a bother. Sorting all the smells, I mean. For one thing that's what I do when I sleep, sort everything I've smelled during the day under the correct label. The dog smells are especially important to keep track of, and that was just what knocked me flat that first week in New York.

There are almost as many dogs as people, you see. At least in Greenwich Village; we normally walked only a few blocks to start with, right across Seventh Avenue and further west down toward the Hudson River, but by the beard of the prophet, I'm just saying, there was hardly a square foot that wasn't already scent marked. And you really do want to read the 'news'.

By and by I got to ride in a taxi. Two or three times a week, Seventh Avenue straight up to Central Park. The idea was to be out early, because after nine o'clock philosophers, I mean dogs, aren't allowed to be off-leash in the park. Silly, if you ask me, but it was lovely up there in those early morning hours, lots of other pooches that smelled of one thing or another and with whom you could exchange opinions. One time I was bitten by a poodle; I hope my ancestors aren't reading this. Real lion dogs use poodles to clean their ears with. Another time I misjudged an elegant leap over a fence and got a gash in my rear end. This resulted in six stitches and just as many staples at a veterinarian's on Hudson Street. A painful story all over.

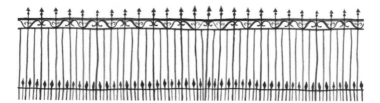

Before we left Central Park in the mornings we usually had breakfast at a café up there, and then we schlepped homeward along the Hudson. No talk of a taxi this time. I would have liked some collective bargaining about this, it was a miserably long and boring hike, but the man and the woman wouldn't hear of it.

Nelson, that lazy cad, never went on walks. He stayed at home in the apartment and in the back courtyard. That was also where he fell in love with the neighbour cat. She was at least ten years older than him, and besides that Nelson, like myself, is castrated. I tried to explain a few facts of life to him,

I really did, but love is blind. At its worst it was five o'clock in the morning when that idiot sat there meowing and pining for his sweetheart. It was after a few such weeks that Nelson had to go home to Sweden. Enough said about cats.

As far as same-species friends are concerned, I had two in New York. One was an introvert grey foxhound whose name was Elvis. In terms of philosophers he didn't measure up to more than approximately Leibniz. The other was more of a laugh, a black puggle (his father was a pug, his mother a beagle, I think; they mix dogs like they mix cocktails in America), and at least it was possible to exchange a few thoughts with him. His name was Max and when he moved at top speed he charged around like a drunken antique rococo dresser. When I took one step he took ten, the poor thing, and when he was going to pee sometimes he lifted his leg so high that he fell over.

I left Manhattan now and then during the two years I lived there – Long Island, the Catskills and Adirondacks, for example – but it's the good smells around James Walker Park, along Seventh Avenue,

Hudson Street and Greenwich Street that left the strongest impressions of New York in my canine head.

But then one day it was moving time again. Furniture disappeared, bags were packed and before I knew it once more I was sitting in one of those dog cages at an airport.

Surely, we're off to Africa this time, I thought, but there I was mistaken.

GOTLAND, MY RELATIONSHIP TO RABBITS

The island of Furilden is somewhat smaller than Manhattan and not inhabited by people. It is inhabited by rabbits. Primarily at least. They are small and quick and run in zigzags. To start with I chased them, or an occasional one anyway, despite my guardians' protests. Here you can clearly see that I'm a lion dog and not a rabbit dog. It was pointless to even get anywhere close to one of those little blighters, and if by chance you

did, it always slipped into a hole much too small for a sturdy specimen like myself.

Conclusion: rabbits aren't worth the trouble. Besides, I'm a pacifist – have I mentioned that? There are also sheep and cows and a flock of hens here, but we all associate like gentlemen under peaceful conditions.

The man and the woman are in the process of building a house on this island, but it never seems to be finished. The first summer we lived in a cabin of approximately ten square metres, but I had no objection. I've always liked cramped spaces. The man and the woman swam in the sea every single morning too, but I want no part of that. Standing on the shore and guarding them is more than enough.

Another difference between Manhattan and Rute, as the parish is called, is that there are fewer dogs here. When you go for a walk, which I'm glad to say we do a couple of times a day, and come upon a stain, it almost always turns out that I'm the one who made it. Earlier in the day or some other day.

On the east side is a meadow, my favourite haunt; I think it must be a bit reminiscent of the savannahs of Africa. When we get here I always rush around like a bat out of hell, the grass is tall and rubs so nicely against my belly. I even chase sticks that the man or the woman throw, a pastime that I otherwise don't contend with. In this I resemble my namesake Søren to a tee, as he didn't like running and fetching things that people threw either. Fetching them with your mouth. It's all a bit infantile.

In any event I soon settled in on Furilden, but imagine my surprise when one beautiful autumn day I was stuffed into the car along with the man and the woman and a lot of baggage and we wended our way southward.

Two days and almost two thousand kilometres later we were in London.

KENSINGTON GARDENS. PANEGYRIC TO A PARK, ET CETERA

Kensington Gardens is a park. I mention this for those who are not so well travelled. Parks in particular are among the finest things that humans have accomplished here on Earth. Civilized nature: by the way, that is a description that fits myself quite well, when I think on it.

London is a city. It is just as big as New York, but there is one important difference. In New York you almost always have to be on a leash, and this applies to Leonbergers, wolfhounds, dachshunds, philosophers, everyone; in London you never have to be on a leash. Except when there are swans in the vicinity, for some reason, and there rarely are.

So we moved into an apartment five minutes away from that park: Kensington Gardens. It's wonderfully large and it's connected to another big open area: Hyde Park. Although Kensington Gardens is the best. I would maintain that of all the places I've been dragged to during my first five years, this is at the top of the list. With all due respect to Central Park in New York, other parks and various forests. We walk here every morning and afternoon, at least an hour every time. I pee a few times outside Orme's Lodge to let it be known that I've arrived. Do the other, you know what, next to some bushes a bit to the left and then I take off across The Broad Walk, through the tall grass and under the ancient trees with owl chicks and parakeets and God knows what, head southeast down toward the Serpentine, that is, and I see so many pleasant acquaintances that half would be enough. Most of them worldly-wise pacifists and everyday philosophers, but also with an interest in the physical side. Well, now I don't mean that biological business – but just wrestling, you see: the rushing and chasing and tumbling and nipping, that's what I'm referring to. That's what I like, I'm not ashamed to admit it. A dog's gotta do what a dog's gotta do, as a sympathetic boxer pointed out when we were lying there catching our breath the other day.

That business with Gotland isn't over, however, I've come to that conclusion.

Sometimes we commute back there, always by car as it turns out, and I must say that's preferable to flying. We drive under the Channel between England and France. Folkestone to Calais, through the tunnel, where I'm lying on my sheepskin in a car on a train. Haha, my ancestors' progeny can't even imagine that as they wander across the plains of Africa in search of the lions that have fled.

Although at this point in time we are on a moor in the county of Somerset. The man and I. This is what I was getting at. We drove here from London almost a week ago, the man has new hiking boots, it's spring and we've been walking this way and that across Exmoor for three days now. I've lost one or two kilos in weight, but it's a magnificent moor. Warm and lovely weather too and jam-packed with interesting smells. Not many trees either, extensive view mostly, just like on the savannah. I do best in open landscapes, that's an old Rhodesian proverb that I absorbed with my mother's milk.

But it wasn't about the smells and the view that I was going to tell. I am fully aware that most of my readers don't care a bit about smells and views. To be prosaic.

THE MAN ON THE HEATH

This happened yesterday, you see.

After a traditional breakfast we set off. By traditional I mean Royal Canin Boxer 26 for me (that's almost the only thing I eat), coffee, juice and yogurt for the man. We brought a packed lunch: more coffee, sandwiches and fruit for him, a fistful of liver treats for myself (I only get two proper meals a day, one in the morning, the other in the evening; I usually finish them off in half-a-minute flat). Water for both of us, of course, but the moor is crisscrossed by a number of streams, so actually that wasn't necessary.

I peed as usual when we had come across the brook, simply to report that I was on the move, and did number two in the shade of a low stone wall a few hundred metres later. The weather was radiant, I could see, lots of interesting but still diffuse scents drifted in with the warm wind from the sea. We had decided to go west this particular day. Previously we had gone east and south. The inn where we are staying is called Whetton Farm; it's located almost in the middle of the moor, so you can actually take off in any direction at all without having to run into distracting settlements. Exmoor is actually in the same class as Kensington Gardens – it feels a little mean for an urban philosopher, I mean dog, to have to admit this, but one shouldn't hold back on the truth.

The man disappeared after about half an hour. It may seem hard to understand that someone can disappear in open terrain, but he has a talent for getting lost. Nothing to make a fuss about, however; I know that he usually finds his way home and there were a number of other hikers out on the moor, so he could always ask the way if it came to that. Besides, he was the one with the map; no, I didn't feel the least bit worried about him.

Instead I followed an unusually interesting scent up an extended slope. To start with I wasn't really clear about what this concerned, but the closer I got to the crown, where a typical ancient, semi-collapsed stone cairn was outlined against the lightly cloud-fluffed sky, the more certain I became.

Meatballs.

No doubt about it. Possibly with notes of fried egg, but that was beside the point. If parks are number one in the human race's contributions to development, then meatballs are number two. This particular morning I was almost inclined to reverse the order. I picked up speed. Tally-ho, tally-ho!

He was sitting leaned against a stone on the other side of the crown. A brown backpack was beside him, and it was from there the aromas emanated. I stopped at a distance of about twenty metres without making myself known and looked around. Below us the moor spread out in extended hollows and ridges, all sloping down toward the sea, which could be made out as a blue line over by the horizon. I'd had it in my nostrils of course for a long time, that salt-tinged, vaguely promising scent, but still could not help being enchanted by the visual experience. It was so lovely in the morning light that for a second it almost surpassed the meatballs.

But only for a second. I cast a glance at the man. He was a contrast to the surrounding landscape, truly a contrast. I noticed at once that something was not quite right about him; we philosophers, sorry,

psychologists, pick up on such things at once. It takes only a fraction of a second for us to read a person's mood, and the person who was now sitting a little way from me – and who had not yet become aware of my presence – was not a happy person. Despite the landscape, the lovely weather, the meatballs.

Not happy at all. I observed him a little while longer before I started to approach him. In his mid-thirties, as far as I could tell. Dressed in typical hiking clothes: heavy boots, trousers of some sturdy material, knitted sweater and a windbreaker that he had taken off and set beside him.

He was lean, and had dark hair with a few streaks of grey. His face was weather-beaten with a couple of days' stubble and he had deep-set eyes – and all of it embedded in a cloud of sorrow. It's just that aura that we dogs discover, and in this case I understood that I was dealing with one of those depressed and depressing people of which there are so many in our time.

He sat there staring blankly ahead, out over the beautiful moor, and he didn't notice me until I was no more than two metres away. He turned his head and gave me a vacant look. I stopped, looked away and turned my withers to show that I had peaceful intentions.

'Come and sit down,' he said, patting his hand on the ground. I noticed that he spoke with a certain Mersey accent. Like John Lennon, more or less. You may wonder how I understood what he was saying; I do have some aptitude for languages, and we had been in England for some time by now.

I gave him a noncommittal nod, and turned around to mark my territory, before I took a place beside him. He stroked me over the neck. I politely sniffed at his hand.

He sighed a few times but let his arm stay resting on my back. I settled into a better position, so that he would understand that I didn't intend to abandon him.

'I wish I were a dog,' he said.

You don't know what you're talking about, I thought. On a different note, what's your name?

'My name's Trevor,' he said. 'Just think how heavy life can be on a beautiful day like this.'

What is it that happened? I wondered. He took a bottle out of the backpack and drank a little water.

Asked if I wanted any. I looked away and he put back the bottle.

'She left me for someone else,' he said. 'Can you imagine? She left me for that blasted Bertram from Leeds.'

That's life, I thought. If you lose one, there are plenty of fish in the sea.

'Such is life,' Trevor went on, sighing again. 'I know they say there's plenty of fish in the sea. But that doesn't help in my case. Betsy's the one I want. No one else. You know what I mean?'

I turned my head and licked his hand.

'Thanks,' he said. 'What does Bertram have that I don't, anyway?'

I didn't answer. For a moment the alluring aromas from the backpack were almost making me dizzy. He sat quietly for half a minute.

'He's stooped over and has bad breath. Bets on the horses and is generally unreliable. What does she see in him?'

Humans are a mystery, I thought, closing my eyes.

'Women are a damned mystery to me,' Trevor observed. 'Do you know what I've decided to do?'

I raised one eyelid and looked at him.

'I intend to kill myself. Put a bullet in my forehead. That's why I'm sitting here. I have a revolver there in the backpack.'

Wouldn't it be better to shoot that Bertram from Leeds? I thought.

'Actually, I ought to shoot that damned Bertram,' said Trevor. 'But if I do, everyone's going to know that I'm the one who did it. I'll end up in prison and Betsy will hate me forever. No, then I'd rather be dead.'

I thought a moment. We sat quietly, observing the landscape and the light clouds out over the sea. Then I put my head in his lap. You should get a dog, I thought.

A quick smile passed over Trevor's face. 'Thanks,' he said, stroking my cheek carefully. 'You know, I really ought to get myself a dog instead. That would be a consolation.'

I licked his hand.

'Would you like a meatball?'

I raised my head and gave him a lick on the mouth too. He stuck his hand down in the backpack and took out a meatball. Nodded at me and stuffed it in my mouth.

Oh, blessedness. I put my head in his lap again and thought that you really don't get full on a single meatball.

'Do you want another one?'

Sometimes we dogs have a hard time really showing how much we appreciate faithful, true friendship. Yes, of course some small dogs are good at fawning and yelping and showing off, but that real, manly friendship, which was in the process of developing between me and Trevor, yes, it's like it needs to be handled differently. I looked at him with my dark, wise eyes and licked my mouth. Tried to smile, but that's not something that comes naturally to me. In any event he put his hand down in the backpack and gave me another meatball.

Oh, double blessedness. But it's not really enough to fill you up.

To make a long story a bit shorter, I stayed there in the sunshine with Trevor for a really long time. We conversed and socialized and philosophized as the sun followed its course, and when every single meatball was eaten up – plus two fried eggs – we kept each other company back to the inn.

'I'll be damned,' he said as we stood out on the yard and said goodbye to each other. 'Tomorrow I'm going to a kennel to get myself a pooch. I don't care about Betsy, thank you very much.'

Just then the man came back from the moor. Exactly as I'd assumed, he had found the way on his own. He and Trevor conversed for a while, and later that evening they had dinner together at the inn. I was lying on the floor under their table and heard Trevor's story one more time. How he was sitting up there by the tower under a cloud of dark thoughts, how he had cursed Betsy and Bertram from Leeds and the meagerness of life – and how I came to him like something sent from above. He truly did not mince words, that Trevor, and I think they shared a few pints besides.

'Yes, sometimes I also think he was sent from above,' the man agreed, beaming contentedly, while for once he stuck his hand down under the table and gave me a bite of something, I think it was goose, or possibly duck. 'I can't really imagine life without him.'

There he spoke from the heart, I'll be the first to testify to that. Thanks, I thought. After the woman, you really are number one.

AFTER-PARTY

So much for that about yesterday. Now it's today, we are still at Exmoor in the county of Somerset and it's time for an afternoon nap. You must cultivate your good habits and even if I'm not wandering in a dark wood, I have probably arrived at the middle of my life's journey anyway. Five and a half years approximately, and it is my pious hope that I still have a number of stages on life's way left. *Wovon man nicht reden kann, darüber muss man schweigen*, as the saying goes. ('Whereof one cannot speak, thereof one must be silent.')

That nap is meant to take place on the man's bed, and I think I've earned it. Writing philosophical tracts takes a lot out of you.

II. **Further Stages on Life's Way**
(2009–14)

Including: *The Woman in the Forest*
— A Morality Tale

ON FOG, HORSES AND A PUB

As it was, life went on.

For a dog, and perhaps for a philosopher, it may be hard to distinguish one day from another. Especially if you live in the same place the whole time, take more or less the same walks and eat the same food. As far as the latter is concerned, here we find a decisive difference between bipeds and us quadrupeds; in general the bipeds get larger, more varied food portions. They can eat and talk nonsense for hours, to be brutally honest, while we starving wretches have to lie under the table and try to fill up on their words and smells.

But I accept the situation as it is – I always have. In general my considerate guardians have had a tendency not to live in the same place all that long, I've already touched on that, so I can't complain about that circumstance anyway. It turned out, for example, that the business with the English moor was not a one-time phenomenon, as I might have thought.

On the contrary, for several years (I think, I have a slight handicap where time calculations are concerned), my place of residence shifted between Kensington Gardens in London, the lovely surroundings on Gotland and a desolate but pleasant place on a moor. The village of Winsford, located in the county of Somerset, or possibly Devon. England, in any event, for those of you who aren't geographers.

And by and by a couple of places in Stockholm. I will return to that.

It was mostly the man and I who stayed out there on the Exmoor heath, and for some reason it was never summer. Fog and rain, though. Wind and mud and plenty of time. In the house where we lived there was another dog of a philosophical nature, a labrador by the name of Haka, and even if he was a bit mature we often took long, meaningful walks over the moor. He taught me a few things. That it's not worth the effort to eat a pheasant. One mustn't let oneself be fooled by the fact that they are easy to catch. They must be the most simple-minded creatures on Earth and are made up of only three components: feathers, splintery bones and squawks. And the bones easily get stuck in your throat. Haka confided that he had to go to the vet twice because of just that. He also said he had seen a pheasant cock keep screeching half an hour after he'd bitten it to death. But there I think he may have dissembled a bit, the good Haka. The English like to tell tales; this applies to all of them, with or without tails.

'So leave them pheasants be,' he summarized. Naturally we spoke English during our walks; Haka had lived in the same house and same country his whole life and didn't know any other language.

Of course one can't eat horses either, possibly as a philosopher, but absolutely not as a dog. I think it was on that moor that I first made the acquaintance of these wise animals, and I immediately came to appreciate their dignified and friendly nature. On the moor they are also completely liberated from people; Haka and I often joined up with their group and listened to their stories about the free life on Exmoor. Nowadays and in the past. Much later I became acquainted with a couple of other nags and if I remember to I will write a few lines about them too.

The man was occupied with some kind of writing

project while we lived in the fog above Winsford. When we weren't out wandering around he usually sat at his desk and looked worried, as he usually does when he's working, while I lay on an extremely pleasant couch and recovered. Although in the evenings we gladly trotted on down to the pub in the village. 'Muddy Paws Welcome,' a sign said on the door, and it truly was an excellent place. There was a thick rug covering the floor where you could dry off your muddy paws, a warm and lovely coal fire in a corner, as well as a bowl of treats for four-legged creatures behind the bar. I don't think I ever felt as satisfied and philosophical as when I lay there, warm, full and contented, while the man had dinner, talked with the villagers, and had a couple of pints of something called Exmoor Ale.

'That's a hell of a nice dog,' I often heard the other patrons say, and I gladly agreed, without making a big show of it. Just a couple of thumps of the tail, to show that I appreciated the compliment.

It was another matter of course to then make our way homeward in the dark, in the rain and uphill, but everything has its time.

BACK TO THE HOMELAND.
STOCKHOLM. MELVIN

By and by it was time to leave Great Britain and move back to Sweden. The man had finished writing his book from the moor, and the woman had started working as a doctor in Stockholm.

Stockholm is the capital of the kingdom of Sweden. I have learned a few things over the years. We came to live in Old Town, which is utterly devoid of green patches but has reasonably interesting smells anyway thanks to all the philosophers, I mean dogs, who live in the alleys. The old chestnut tree at the little square, for example, where we all lift our legs during the morning walk across the cobblestones, and sometimes you're able to drag the human at the other end of the leash with you into the café there. If you're a gourmet dog, you always get a meatball or two at that place. This is a type of urban civilization that I can really relate to.

Imagine my astonishment when one day I got a cousin. It was a silly little puppy more reminiscent of a four-legged hen than a dog: off-white, fluffy, furry, eager to the point of hysteria, scatterbrained, pop-eyed and totally unphilosophical. Approximately a tenth of my weight when I first met him, yes, my Lord, it was hard to understand what use he would be. His name was Melvin, that's all, and his guardian was somehow related to mine. In lineal descent, I believe it's called, which was why I was forced to associate with the four-legged hen. 'Breed?', a friend of order will ask. None at all: probably composed of spare parts left over.

But life is a strange invention. I put young Melvin in his place, of course, firmly but not overly hard. I believe I've mentioned that I'm a pacifist? And even if

to start with I thought he was a completely untrainable cousin, he learned. Quickly even, and he turned out to be really clever. One shouldn't judge the hen by its hairs or the book by its cover and I soon realized that I actually liked the little rascal. Especially on Gotland we associated regularly, even if he had to stand stretched out on his hind legs to be able to reach up, lick me on the cheek and declare his esteem. Yes, we lived a lovely, free, open-air life there in the summers, and at night we often slept together back to back on the excellent round pad that the man and the woman had acquired during our years in New York.

So not a bad word about Melvin. On the contrary, considered as a philosopher he probably reminded me most of Descartes: 'I am, therefore I exist', or something like that. As the attentive reader has perhaps noted, I have started to slip a bit between present and past tense in my presentation; presumably that is due to the fact that nowadays I'm dead. I will return to that matter toward the end.

But it is still a couple of years until then and first I want to tell about a little red house in an extremely nice park.

KATARINAVÄGEN. SÖDER.
VITA BERGEN. THE WOMAN

Even if you usually have your nose firmly lodged on the tarmac, you can't help noticing that Stockholm is a beautiful city. It is especially beautiful if you toddle up a long street called Katarinavägen in a part of the city called Söder, because it's in the south. I mention this if there were to be a doubtful reader or other sitting in a village in the far north or perhaps on the island of Öland, wondering whether it may be worth the effort to take a trip to the capital.

It *is* worth the effort. Even if you are a philosophical dog who has his youth behind him, you realize that there is a point in making your way up Katarinavägen every day. Lifting your head and looking out toward Djurgården, Skeppsholmen, Old Town and the whole enchilada. Like Strindberg did a hundred and fifty years ago. I know that the man thinks the same, because every morning we always walked a little bit slower right there.

The goal for our more or less daily walks (especially

during the winter months when we weren't on Gotland as often) was a little red wooden shack in a park called Vitabergsparken. You see, the man had decided that he needed some kind of workplace, because our little apartment in Old Town was too cramped for his great spirit. I'm not sure that he thought in just those terms but it's all the same, that old red house was furnished in any event with all that an author requires. A desk, a chair, some bookshelves and last but not least: a leather couch! Hallelujah, I always thought when we were finally there after half an hour out in the open on a windy, rainy November morning. A human's best friend is a dog, that's obvious, but a dog's best friend is a leather couch.

There was a big open fireplace besides. A crackling fire, the man at the desk, the philosopher on the couch, need I say more? Yes, perhaps that the man used to move over to the couch after an hour or so. Then you had to squeeze in together, but we four-legged philosophers have nothing against a little warm crowding, so there was never any problem.

Right next to the house with the crackling fire, the author and the philosopher on the couch was

something called an off-leash area. It's actually quite nice: big and a bit rocky and with a good deal of vegetation, not at all like certain cramped asphalt patches I've encountered here and there during my roving life. Off-leash areas exist so that dogs can run loose and socialize with each other without being attached to a person.

Now over the years I have become more accustomed to not being attached to anything, so actually I had no need of those kinds of small enclosures. But it did happen of course that I made a visit if the weather was suitable and there appeared to be an interesting philosopher or two on the scene. For example, I associated happily for a while with Bruno – a ridgeback like myself, inclined toward the French, slightly speculative school, Sartre and such – and Madeleine, an awfully nice-looking female boxer with whom I gladly would have paired if I'd been a few years younger and still had my testicles. (They disappeared several years ago under murky circumstances – have I brought that up?)

Although Vita Bergen is of course nicest outside the enclosed patch. It is green and bushy and rolling, and say what you will about the man and the woman, they have at least managed to find lovely surroundings for me: Central Park, Kensington Gardens, Exmoor, Gotland, Vita Bergen, Old Town with the meatball café. And soft furniture, as mentioned. It could have been worse, much worse, and I realize that most philosophers live under considerably more difficult circumstances than I have. You should have the sense to be grateful.

If there is anyone who could bear to read this far, it may be that they have acquired a slight misunderstanding. In that case it would be that the man is the most significant person in my canine life. It's not that way at all. He's quite all right, but it's the woman who is number one. No doubt about it. A philosophical dog knows such things. Don't ask me how. Sometimes they tested the matter: we might be out wandering in some forest, all three of us, and then suddenly they would go off in separate directions. I knew immediately of course that it was best to follow the woman, but would always stand there a moment anyway in feigned hesitation before I left the man to his fate. Out of consideration, of course,

I wanted to let him believe anyway that I had to think a bit before deciding.

THE WOMAN IN THE FOREST – A MORALITY TALE

I have no idea what in the world *morality* means, but I like the word. It is of course from the man that I've learned the art of tossing out expressions you don't really have the hang of, so I blame him. But now it's high time to tell the curious episode with a peculiar woman and her even more peculiar pet. It all played out on the fair island of Gotland.

Summer morning. Sun and clouds in a lovely mixture. Mild breeze from the sea, cuckoos calling in the east and not a worry as far as my nose could reach. A day made for lying in the shade and philosophizing, in other words. It was soon clear, however, that the man and the woman had other plans. A walk.

Long walk to be doubly sure, one could assume that because both of them had outfitted themselves with tennis shoes, water bottles and American baseball caps. For my part I have never had anything against wandering in forest and field, even if my youthful enthusiasm has declined with the years. Melvin, however, is a veritable opponent of most types of excursions. His legs are so short that he has to take four or six steps when I take one, and besides his impractical hen-fur means that everything imaginable gets stuck in it, so that he usually has to go for a bath and grooming afterwards. When Melvin is wet he looks like he drowned several years ago.

We quadrupeds naturally had no choice. The man and the woman set off with decisive steps and assumed optimism. Melvin and I took it calmly. Made sure to stay twenty or thirty metres behind and slow down the pace as best we could.

We must have been trotting for about fifteen minutes when we came to a familiar junction. Our guardians took off to the left without looking around. Melvin stopped.

'By all moose antlers, holy macaroni,' he said. (He often maintains that his name was Davy Crockett in a previous life and that he talked like that.) 'They intend to walk around the whole northern half. I'm so over this walk.'

'It doesn't look good,' I noted.

'I'm tired,' said Melvin. 'My legs feel like half-thawed fish fingers.'

'We haven't walked that far,' I pointed out.

'Ten thousand steps for my part,' said Melvin. 'It's not easy to be a rather little dog in these circumstances.'

'*Very* little,' I corrected him. 'You are a very little dog, Melvin, don't imagine anything else.'

He didn't respond to that. Instead he rose up on his rear legs to get a slightly better overview. Half a metre above the ground or so.

'I know a short cut,' he said, waving his paw toward an opening between two spruce trees. 'If we go in here we can meet up with them over by the fishing village and save several kilometres.'

I looked around and thought. Realized that was correct.

'Okay,' I said. 'You're quite clever for a hen-hound.'

We hadn't gone very far on the beaten-down path before we caught sight of something red sticking out next to a fallen tree.

'What's that?' said Melvin. 'Looks like a . . . '

'Shoe,' I filled in. 'Yes, truly, it's a sort of pump or whatever it's called.'

'I think they're called pumps,' said Melvin. 'At least if there are two of them.'

But this one was all alone. A woman's shoe with high heel, that is. Red and shiny and nice, I thought that it couldn't have been lying there all that long. Almost looked like it came straight from the store and landed here in the moss. Melvin went up and nosed at it.

'Woman,' he said. 'Dark and a little plump. In her forties if I'm not mistaken. No stockings or pantyhose.'

I went up and checked. Determined that this was presumably correct.

'Eight hours,' I added. 'It hasn't been lying here any longer than that. Probably less. What do we do?'

'We go on,' said Melvin.

So we did.

The path wound on through the forest. We did too. We had walked here before and the scents got stronger with every metre. After a while we made our next discovery.

'Look there,' said Melvin. 'It looks like a . . . '

'Bicycle,' I said. 'It wasn't lying here yesterday.'

'How do you know that?' said Melvin.

'Went with the man on a run,' I said. 'We ran past here. You were snoring behind the woodshed, I seem to recall.'

'That was the right thing to do,' said Melvin, sniffing the bicycle, which was abandoned in a clump of ferns right by the side of the path.

'The same woman?' I asked.

'Without a doubt,' said Melvin. 'The mystery deepens.'

We continued in silence and with heightened watchfulness. I spied off to the left, Melvin off to the right. A high-heeled shoe and a bicycle, what could that mean? Whatever this was about, it didn't bode well; we were in agreement on that without having to exchange a word about it.

The path got narrower, the forest more tangled, just like always at this place. The scent of forty-year-old woman increased. Lightly perfumed but not recently. A faint element of alcohol. Cooled sweat.

No, this did not bode well.

I was the one who discovered her. She was leaned up against a tree trunk a dozen metres from the path, wearing a light, slightly soiled summer dress, and it looked as if she was asleep. A short distance from her, almost out on the path where Melvin and I had stopped abruptly, was yet another red, high-heeled woman's shoe. Without wanting to draw hasty conclusions, I connected it with the one we had already encountered.

'Well?' said Melvin. 'So you see.'

'That I do, dear Watson, sorry, I mean Melvin,' I said. 'What do you think about this?'

'I'm not saying anything, so I haven't said anything,' said Melvin. 'But she has a bird on a cord. That's unusual.'

It was correct, I just hadn't noticed it. Even though he is little and pop-eyed he can be really attentive sometimes, young Melvin, I'll give him credit for that. There truly was a green bird sitting on a branch above the lady's head. And there was a cord running

from one of its legs down to her wrist. Still tied as it appeared.

We stood silently awhile and observed the pair.

'She's asleep,' I said. 'That green cuckoo probably is too. Don't you think it's time to wake them?'

'Certainly,' said Melvin, letting out one of his pitiful barks. He sounds more like a duck that's got caught; I've always thought that, but at this point I had stopped pointing it out long ago.

The woman woke up with a start.

'Help!' she cried in terror. 'Where am I? What time is it?'

Take it easy, I thought. You're sitting there. It's a

beautiful summer morning but I have no idea what time it is.

Melvin got up on his rear legs so that he could whisper in my ear.

'Damn. What do you think happened?'

'It will probably be cleared up,' I said. 'Just stay still; people usually talk to dogs if you just cock your head and look friendly.'

We cocked our heads and looked friendly.

'Oh my goodness,' said the woman, rubbing her eyes with her knuckles. 'So I've ended up here. But what nice dogs. Where did you two come from? Ouch!'

She touched her foot and I could see that it was swollen and big as a French bulldog.

'Ouch, ouch, ouch,' she moaned. 'Of course, now I remember. I twisted my foot last night, that's why I'm sitting here.'

And what were you doing out in the forest in the middle of the night? I wondered, looking at her a little challengingly. Just that look that usually gets people to talk.

'It was that darned Captain Silver,' she said with

a sigh, gesturing up toward the green bird that only now seemed to have come to life. 'He flew off, that naughty parrot!'

'SHIP AHOY! THIS IS CAPTAIN SILVER SPEAKING!' the bird suddenly shrieked in a loud voice, so that both Melvin and I backed up a couple of steps. Melvin started sounding like a duck again.

'Don't be afraid. He's a talking parrot,' the woman explained. 'He flew away last night just because that idiot Arne let him loose.'

I nodded a little vaguely. Melvin nodded even more vaguely.

'Like this, see,' the woman continued, carefully straightening up against the tree trunk. It looked like she was in pain. 'Arne is my crazy brother-in-law. We had a little gathering and he consumed way too much mead. He got drunk and crazy and in the middle of the night he let Captain Silver out through the window. Ouch, my foot!'

'I took off after him at once of course,' the woman said with a sigh. 'He's not used to being outdoors and wouldn't survive very long on his own. I've had him for sixteen years and I love him!'

Love is blind, I thought, casting a glance up toward the bird, who sat twisting and turning his yellow–red head (the rest was green, as stated) and looking remarkable.

'More than my husband, actually,' she added. 'It would have been much better if both he and Arne had jumped from the balcony instead, as drunk and unruly as they were.'

'She was probably not completely sober herself either,' Melvin whispered in my ear. 'She reeks of old whiskey.'

'Gotland mead is reminiscent of diluted whiskey,' I whispered back. After all, I had several more years and somewhat more experience under my belt than my little cousin.

And so then she set out on a parrot hunt? I thought. On a bicycle? In the middle of the night?

'Yes, what should I do?' the woman exclaimed, throwing out her arms. 'I got on the bike and took off after him. In the middle of the night! I had to rescue him! My name is Mrs Blomgren, by the way.'

'WHAT AN AMAZING ASS!' Captain Silver yelled. 'HALLELUJAH!'

Oh boy, I thought. High-heeled shoes on a bike in the dark! Stupid.

'High-heeled shoes on a bike in the dark,' Mrs Blomgren observed with another sigh. 'That's not a good combination. I got a bead on that rapscallion anyway and it was fine until he flew in over the forest here. But I had no choice. I followed him on that darned path as best I could. Lost a shoe, fell over and had to leave the bike, and then ...'

'She started running and twisted her foot,' Melvin whispered excitedly in my ear.

' ... I started running with just one shoe. That's not the easiest, I must say, and right when I got hold of that noisy bird I stepped wrong and twisted my foot!'

I wondered how in the world she managed to capture the bird, but didn't bother to ask. In any event, Captain Silver was now sitting properly attached to the cord that ran between his foot and the woman's wrist.

'WHAT A BABE!' he bawled. 'CAPTURED BY A STORM WIND! FINGAL IS A PILE OF SHIT!'

I cast a glance at Melvin and thought that this walk we would probably remember, both of us. And who could Fingal be?

But now the woman, whose name was thus Mrs Blomgren (and whom I suddenly seemed to recall having encountered previously in the parish, although not with this aroma of old perfume, stale alcohol and French bulldog foot) started crying in despair. 'Ouch, ouch, ouch,' she sobbed. 'I can't get out of here without help. I can't put any weight on my foot, I'm going to sit here until I freeze to death!'

I thought that was an unnecessarily pessimistic prognosis, because the weather was beautiful and surely twenty degrees Celsius in the air. But I realized anyway that a clear and resolute intervention was what was required.

'Listen up now, Melvin,' I said. 'I know that you're not much of a gentleman, but we really ought to intervene and straighten this out. This actually concerns a damsel in distress. A dog's gotta do what a dog's gotta do.'

'DAMNED LOUDMOUTHS!' the parrot shrieked. 'THIS IS CAPTAIN SILVER SPEAKING!'

Melvin nodded seriously and started chewing on a pine cone. This was naturally not the time to chew pine cones, but I let him be. Now and forever he is who he is.

'All right,' he said at last, settling down at a proper distance from Mrs Blomgren and Captain Silver. 'You find the long-legged ones, I'll stand guard!'

So it was too, to make a long story short. I took off along the path and just as Melvin had calculated I ran into the man and the woman near the old stone cabin, where in the past fishermen would spend the night. From what I've understood.

'I see, there you are, my friend,' the woman said, stroking me over the neck. 'But what have you done with Melvin Melvinsson?'

They usually call him that, maybe so that he will seem a little bigger if he gets a surname. For my part I don't need a last name (Kierkegaard I use only as a pseudonym when I'm writing books), I'll be noticed anyway.

Follow me so I won't have to explain, I thought, and started trotting off slowly in the same direction from which I'd come.

Turned my head to check that they got the point.

'He wants us to follow him,' the woman said, who is probably the cleverer of the two. 'Something must have happened.'

And so we trudged back through the forest, all three of us.

The situation was unchanged when we reached Melvin, Mrs Blomgren and Captain Silver.

'Oh boy,' said the man. 'What happened here?'

'CHEERS AND WELCOME!' Captain Silver shrieked. 'TAKE OFF YOUR SHOES DAMN IT!'

'Thank God,' Mrs Blomgren exclaimed sitting there in pain, leaning against her tree trunk. 'I'm sitting here and can't do a thing. So was it the dog that fetched you? What a clever pooch!'

I don't really like being called 'pooch,' but 'clever' compensated for that. I got a big hug from the woman and two liver treats from the man. Melvin got up of course and received the same allotment.

Mrs Blomgren told her story and approximately in the middle the man took off to arrange transport. He returned quite soon with a wheelbarrow, they bedded it down with a bunch of twigs and moss, and then Mrs Blomgren got to take a seat in it. It was rather awkward bumping along on the path, but soon we were out on the old military road and then they picked up rather good speed. Melvin probably would have preferred to ride in the wheelbarrow too, but with both Mrs Blomgren and the parrot it was more than full.

'Thank God you came,' Mrs Blomgren repeated at regular intervals. 'And what an outstanding dog you have . . . yes, the little pop-eyed one too, of course.'

'I know,' said the man. 'But stay still now so we don't tip over.'

'SHIP AHOY!' Captain Silver called. 'WHAT A BABE!'

I thought that I was happy that the man and the woman hadn't gone in for parrots, it would have been trying in the long run.

Before we knew it we were home again and the man drove off with Mrs Blomgren and Captain Silver in the car. I assume that the destination was the husband and brother-in-law. Or the emergency room perhaps? A foot that looks like a French bulldog is not anything to play with.

The woman said that anyway and she's a doctor.

So what about the morality? the inquisitive reader perhaps will ask. Shucks, I don't know. I did say that I didn't really have the hang of that word.

III. Final Stages on Life's Way
(2014)

Including: *Dog Heaven*

REYR AND SAFIR.
INFIRMITIES AND OLD AGE

The summer of 2014 would be my last.

That same summer two new, equally unexpected and welcome friends came to us on Gotland.

Their names were Reyr and Safir and they came flying from a little island realm called Iceland. Now I don't mean that they came flying on their own, that wouldn't have worked because these were two horses without a trace of wings. No, the woman travelled to that island out in the Atlantic and bought them, and then they got to fly in an airplane to Sweden, and by and by they ended up on a completely different island.

I'm sure it was not a pleasant journey. When I met them for the first time they looked skinny and depressed, but after a few weeks at a lovely place called Gåsemora they had filled out properly and seemed to be doing great.

Before long they came home to us and grazed around our house, and I got to know them very well.

If there are any animals in Our Lord's pasture that can philosophize, then that would be horses. Perhaps they don't have so many thoughts, but they think big. I explained to them that I had some experience with their way of reasoning from my time at Exmoor, and between chewing (horses eat almost all the time, but at least as much comes out the other end) they told about life on Iceland. It's a completely treeless country, evidently, and for that reason there aren't many dogs either. Nothing to lift your leg against, if you know what I mean.

Safir in particular often used to stand there between chews and look out over the sea. I thought maybe he was homesick, but when I asked him one day he simply answered that it was the same sea here as there and that the grass tasted more or less the same.

Both the man and the woman spoke Swedish with our Icelanders, but we quadrupeds kept to *North-Dachshundish* when no humans were around. This is an artificial animal language, invented by the wire-haired Danish phoneticist Jeppe Blixen Jacobsen a hundred years ago or more, and it works just fine in most contexts. At least between philosophers with a tail in northern Europe. And that was of course where we were.

The woman rode Reyr and Safir a fair amount that summer, but the man and I would have no part of that. We like having both feet on the ground (in my case, all four), it's always been that way, but that doesn't mean we didn't appreciate and enjoy the addition to the family.

To start with sometimes I ran alongside when the woman was out on her rides (walk or trot or amble or canter – it's crazy how many ways there are to move along if you're an Icelandic hack), but as summer progressed, I noticed more and more that I didn't feel like it. I got tired, and a treacherous ache had slipped into my joints besides. Unpleasant and intensifying, I would say. It was especially my left-front leg that hurt, and some mornings I could barely get myself up on all fours.

One should bear in mind that at this stage of my life's journey, counted in human years, I had passed eighty by a good margin. I am aware that humans often have a hard time with death, but for us quadrupeds it's the most natural thing in the world. Everything has its time: being born, living, dying.

And everything conceivable in between and in the meantime.

FINITO

When autumn came and it was time to start the winter months in Stockholm, we decided. The man and the woman cried and fumbled for words and put it off, of course, that's the way they are. But when they saw me struggle with the stairs in Old Town and noticed that I preferred to sleep eighteen hours a day, they understood that there was no alternative. I fixed my tired eyes on them and convinced them, it was that simple.

At the end of October I fell asleep for the last time on the woman's lap, with the man hanging over me as if he had a strong desire to go with me on that final journey. They cried rivers, both of them, and when it was over they were almost inconsolable.

But as I've already said a few times: a dog's gotta do what a dog's gotta do.

And when a dog's gotta go, a dog's gotta go.

I don't think I need to explain what I mean.

ON THE OTHER SIDE

So now I go on living up here.

Dog heaven. It's truly not a bad place. In many ways reminiscent of Gotland, actually. Small villages and nature, no cities, but plenty of dogs. There are even cats here. I am neighbours with Haka from Exmoor, and Kastor, my childhood friend from Uppsala.

I am six years old all the time, an ideal age for a dog. You still have your youthful spirit, but also a good measure of wisdom and ability to enjoy the day. Sometimes it rains, but usually the sun is shining – and it is only winter one month a year (so that you don't forget how nice it can be to lie in front of an open fire, farting and philosophizing, like at that pub in Winsford).

I am still a pacifist. Everyone is on this side.

I also keep reasonably good track of them down there on Earth. My mortal remains are buried in two different places not far from the house on Gotland. The woman's favourite place and the man's favourite place. They go there quite often, and as they stand there after they've lit a candle and perhaps said a prayer, it's not particularly difficult to make contact with them. Most recently especially with the man, we've needed to talk a bit to produce these memoirs.

And I tell them that I'm doing just fine in dog heaven and that I'm waiting for them. I'm going to wag my tail and welcome them when that day comes.

Although I think it will be a while. I have a successor and one does hope that he as well as the man and the woman get to live their full measure on Earth. Reyr and Safir too, of course. And Melvin. His name is Hudson, the new four-legged philosopher. He looks like an uncommonly pleasant fox, although a little bigger, and I think he's going to turn out fine.

It's good to know that they are in good hands, I mean paws, in that way, the man and the woman. Without a dog people don't do well.

So that's how it is, it's no more complicated than that, this business of life and death.

But enough said and enough philosophizing. Kastor and Haka are waiting by the gate, we're going for a run. Over and out.

CONCLUDING REMARK

A lick on the mouth to the woman and one to the man too; he's the one who wrote down the latter part of my reflections according to my instructions.

Thanks also to all you readers. If you haven't learned anything, at least you haven't done anything stupid while you've been reading.

Woof-woof from heaven.

Norton Kierkegaard, former canine philosopher